Francesco and his

The Andersen Young Readers Library

OTHER TITLES IN THE ANDERSEN YOUNG READERS LIBRARY

Mischa Damjan

Francesco and his Donkeys

Illustrated by
Mona Ineichen

Translated by
Patricia Crampton

Andersen Press/Hutchinson
London

Andersen Press Ltd.
in association with
Hutchinson Ltd.
3 Fitzroy Square
London W 1

First published in English 1977
This translation ©1977 by Andersen Press Ltd.
Originally published in German as
Francesco und seine Eselchen by K. Thienemanns Verlag,
Stuttgart

Printed in Great Britain
ISBN 0 905478 12 6

Contents

1 A Donkey is Born

The heroine of this story is a shaggy little donkey who lived on the beautiful, sunny island of Corsica.

The baby donkey came into the world in a dark stable on a farm close to the sea. Her mother's name was Trotella, which is an unusual name for a donkey. It means 'skipping girl' and she had been given the name because her high spirits made her skip and frolic when she was young. But now Trotella was a hard-working old donkey and a good mother.

The little donkey was born on a mild, autumn day. Autumn had always been a happy time for the people of the island, especially the farmers, but it was not a happy time for Trotella and her baby.

Autumn brought the precious olives and sweet grapes, ruddy brown chestnuts and juicy oranges—to human beings. But to the mother donkey it brought labour, and to the baby, loneliness.

Only a few days after the birth of the baby donkey, old Dominic came to take Trotella out to work again. She followed him reluctantly, because she had to leave her baby alone in the straw, gazing sadly after her.

Trotella had to pull a heavy beam in

a circle, from early morning to late at night. The beam was attached to an olive press which squeezed the precious oil from the ripe fruit. Just as men or mules once used to turn the little roundabouts at the fair ground, so Trotella turned the olive press day after day. She pulled the heavy beam as if she herself were an engine, walking round and round in a circle, always at the same speed, day in, day out.

To make it easier for her to walk in an endless circle, and also to prevent her from feeling giddy, the farmer tied a cloth over Trotella's eyes. So it was that no one could see the donkey's eyes, and no one knew how sad she was because her baby lay alone and forlorn in the gloomy stable. But Trotella was very sad. She would have liked to stay with her shaggy, long-eared baby, to share her warmth and give her as much milk as she needed.

Unfortunately, the good creature could not do everything at once; she could not look after her baby and work at the olive press all day long.

'She must work, even if she has a baby. After all, she's only a donkey,' said the farmer, her master. And that was why Trotella was so sad.

2 The Baby Escapes

Two weeks later, when Trotella was working at the olive press, Long Ears was lying alone and abandoned as ever in the straw. Sometimes she cast an imploring glance about her, for the stable was gloomy and unfriendly. The little donkey was frightened and longed for her mother. Then she got to her feet, tripped over to the window and tried to look out. But the window was too high for her. Disappointed, she snuffled about until she discovered a sack of hay lying just under

11

the window. The little donkey planted her four feet firmly on it and peered out. There was a wood outside, a green meadow and a single fir tree. And what was in the green meadow? A foal was bounding playfully about and its mother, the brown mare, was watching over it. Even the little rabbits were allowed to be out there, enjoying the sunshine.

Long Ears was feeling still more homesick for her mother. 'I'm the only one that has to be locked in here. Why?' she asked plaintively. The farmer, her master, thought it was a good thing for the little donkey to be locked in the stable, because he was afraid that it might run straight to its mother and disturb her at her important work.

Long Ears went on looking out of the window for some time and then moved away, more lonely and depressed than before. She went to the stable door and kicked it, but it was locked and did not yield to her despairing kicks.

In the end little Long Ears became

very tired. She was still only a very
young donkey. She was suddenly so
tired and desperate that she lay down

in the straw and made a nest for herself. A moment later, she pricked up her ears. Someone had come to the door and was trying to open it. In a flash the little prisoner had buried her head in the straw, thinking that no one would be able to see her. But her ears were both big and long, so they stuck out above the straw and her thin legs and comical little tail gave her away as well. All the same, the little donkey behaved as if she were not there at all. She thought she could not be seen because she herself could see nothing. She scarcely dared to breathe. Once again she heard heavy footsteps; probably the visitor was going off to fetch the key. The little donkey was a valuable piece of property to the farmer and so she was well guarded. When she grew up, she would replace her mother at the olive press.

Then she heard the sound of someone fumbling with the key at the lock. After two or three failures, the key turned in the lock and the door creaked open. In the doorway stood Dominic

the farmhand, in his red, pointed ca
He seemed to think for a moment and
then walked firmly over to the other
corner of the stable, away from the
place where the little donkey was hid-
ing in the straw. Dominic took a big
scythe down from its rail and saun-
tered out again without a glance at the
hidden Long Ears. He had barely gone
out before the little animal raised her
head warily and peeped at the door.
Then she shook herself briskly and
wiggled her long ears, because she
could scarcely see. Wisps of straw
hung in front of her eyes and stuck to
her mouth. When the straw dropped to
the ground, the little donkey saw a
thin beam of sunlight lying across the
straw, gleaming golden in the dark-
ness of the stable. She became curious,
stood up and crept towards the door.

It's open! the little donkey discovered. Old Dominic had obviously
forgotten how important the little donkey was to his master and had not
locked the door behind him. In fact, he
had not even closed it properly!

The donkey listened tensely. There was silence outside. With a little luck, she would soon be with her mother!

The donkey snuffled to herself and listened again, without daring to open the door any wider. But nothing happened and nothing was moving. Suddenly she plucked up courage and pushed the door wider with her head. She peeped out cautiously—no one to be seen—only the brown mare, still watching her foal playing in the meadow. The playful rabbits were still there too, big and small, a whole family of them. Long Ears was not afraid of them. All she feared was human beings; but there was not one of them anywhere in sight. Her heart thumped with excitement. It thumped with joy! And in a flash—the little donkey had gone.

3 Strange Christening

Barely five minutes had passed, and already the escaped donkey was nuzzling her mother's velvet mouth. It was a real donkey's kiss!

Although Trotella's eyes were covered, she immediately recognised her baby from her movements and her smell. She was happy, but she did not stop walking because she was afraid that would spoil her work. Trotella was a sensible and experienced mother.

And what did the little donkey do?

17

She walked along beside her mother,
her head held proudly, and flicked her
constantly with the bushy paintbrush
which was her tail. She could hear

laughter from all sides. The farm-hands in charge of the olive press thought it very funny and laughed and laughed, but that did not worry the little donkey. She was so happy to be with her mother.

Now, sitting on a fence near the press was a sunburnt boy called Francesco, who was watching solemnly. He looked very sad as his eyes followed the shaggy little escaped prisoner, who had already trotted round more than a dozen times, docilely accompanying her mother. Now her little head was dropping lower at every step and her thin legs were quivering more and more. The mother donkey began to feel that her baby was getting tired and she slowed down. At once the bearded farmer came over and cracked his whip.

'Get on, faster!' he shouted. 'There are a lot of olives to be pressed.' The olive oil was very important to the farmers of Corsica.

Trotella hesitated for a moment, in spite of the whip, as if she were not quite sure what to do. Then she quickened her pace again. The little donkey was left further and further behind and gazed miserably after her. She looked very weak but she went on trying to catch up. Unfortunately her little legs were not nearly as strong as the desire in her heart. First she fell to her knees and then to the ground. The farmhands were laughing more loudly than ever, as if it were all an amusing game. Only one old man, who had come to the island from Italy, scratched his head thoughtfully and cried: 'Sfortunata! Sfortunata!'

The men by the olive press were struck by the word and repeated it without laughing. So the little donkey was given her name, Sfortunata, which means simply 'Unlucky'. And since she really was unlucky, the name suited her well. Now the farmhands had stopped laughing. This unusual christening had made them sympathise with the little donkey, but sympathy was not much help to Trotella or to Sfortunata.

Trotella still had to turn the heavy beam in circles, because the farmers were all agreed that a donkey was born to that work.

When Sfortunata fell down, Trotella was aware what had happened to her baby, in spite of her covered eyes. She stopped for an instant beside Sfortunata, lowered her head and looked as if she were about to try to release herself from the leather straps which bound her to the beam. They scolded her violently; they hit her, but she did not move from the spot. Seeing that she was going to be stubborn, the bearded farmer came and poured a jug of cold water over the head of the motionless Sfortunata. To everyone's amazement she heaved herself painfully onto her front legs, and shook her head, her long ears waggling in all directions. The men began to laugh again. They thought it was a great joke to see Sfortunata kneeling there, waggling her ears to and fro. But it was no joke to Sfortunata, Oh no! She was in complete despair. All the same, she tried

21

slowly to get to her feet. At that moment the boy on the fence ran to help her, got her onto her feet, pulled off his shirt and dried her soaking neck with it. Then he led her slowly back to the stable.

4 Francesco and Sfortunata

Francesco sat in the straw, thinking. Beside him lay the exhausted Sfortunata, gazing wretchedly towards the door of the stable, beyond which her mother was still dragging the heavy beam of the press in circles. Francesco looked at Sfortunata lovingly. He had lost his heart to the unlucky donkey at first sight. But Sfortunata was well aware that Francesco was neither a jolly rabbit nor a frolicsome pony, but a small human being. And she knew that she had to beware of human

beings. The closer Francesco came to
her, the deeper she buried herself in
the straw. But he did not hold it

24

against her; he himself had seen them hitting her mother with a whip. 'The farmhands really think it's funny that Sfortunata is so helpless,' thought Francesco furiously and he ran quickly back to the house to fetch milk and bread for Sfortunata.

When he came back to her she refused at first to touch the food. Francesco thought desperately; how could he help Sfortunata? Perhaps he should ask his father to buy another donkey and leave Trotella with her little Sfortunata in the stable? Then mother and daughter could play in the meadow to their heart's content. Sfortunata ought to have a happy life, at least as a young donkey. Later, when she was big and grown-up, she would have to work all day long for the rest of her life. Francesco was dreaming of happy days for his little Long Ears, but his dream soon ended when he realised that his father would laugh at him. Yes, his father was sure to tease him: 'Haven't you learnt anything better in school than being sorry for your donkey?' That was what his father would say, although he was not a bad man at all. He was a farmer, whose only interest in pets was their usefulness to him. These thoughts went round and round in Francesco's head as he sat beside Sfortunata in the straw. He was determined to help her, but how, how?

He looked down at her. She was asleep now and Francesco watched the sleeping donkey thoughtfully for a time. Then he remembered old Thomas. The fisherman was fond of him and always had an answer for Francesco's worries. 'Thomas is sure to help me,' thought Francesco and he decided to go straight to the village. He left the food he had brought for Sfortunata beside her, hoping she would take some when she woke up.

5 The Boy and the Fisherman

When Francesco hurried from the stable Sfortunata was still fast asleep. The little boy got his bicycle out of the barn and raced down to the seashore, to the place where Thomas always sat, mending his boat and his nets.

After a breakneck ride Francesco caught sight of the old fisherman in the distance. He was sitting on the sand, mending a net. A few more kicks at the pedals and the boy who liked things to be fair was sitting beside the old fisherman, who knew so much about life. Francesco poured out his heart to him. The old man smoked his weathered old pipe serenely while he considered. It looked as if he could not see a way out either. His eyes searched the boy's face and he asked kindly, 'Tell me, my boy, why did you decide to come to me?'

'You've been living so long by the great sea, under the broad sky, Thomas, and you know such a lot about everything. You know which wind makes which fish bite. You know why the octopus can live for a long time without water and why the inkfish are poor swimmers. You know all the stars in the sky by name ... and. ...' Francesco stopped and looked into the old man's bearded face. When he saw his kindly smile, he went on bravely, 'I think you even know where to find the most precious pearls in the sea. You *must* know what we can do for Sfortunata, Thomas.'

The old fisherman frowned.

'Do Sfortunata and her children and grandchildren have to go on being

unlucky for ever?' Francesco sighed.
The furrows on Thomas's brow deep-
ened and he said, 'My dear Francesco,

29

if a man doesn't already know when he's young that we human beings have to care for the animals as well as ourselves, then it is generally too late when he's old.'

Francesco knew that the old fisherman was talking about his father and many of the other farmers on the island. He thought sorrowfully of Sfortunata in her gloomy stable.

'Thomas,' said Francesco angrily, 'there's one thing I can't understand. People are kind to mares and stallions and cows and bulls and ducks and geese, but they've only got work and whips and jokes for the donkeys. But donkeys don't ask for anything and they've always helped people. They have driven mills and well wheels, worked on olive presses, pulled heavy carts and taken things to market and they're always patient and obedient. They don't need rich meadows, they're happy with very simple food. They eat the things that grow on stony paths: nettles and thistles and even thorns. They live so very cheaply, Thomas!'

Francesco looked into the fisherman's bearded face and Thomas nodded.

'Then why do the donkeys just get hit and teased? They say donkeys are stupid, but why? Why?'

The old fisherman looked kindly at him, obviously surprised. 'How do you know so much about donkeys?'

'Our teacher told us,' said Francesco impatiently. His thoughts were already back with Sfortunata and he was suddenly convinced that she was awake and frightened.

'They need an engine for the olive press,' muttered the old man, as if his idea were completely impossible.

'An engine! An engine! Of course, that's what we need!' cried Francesco delightedly. But in a moment he was downcast again. An engine cost money, a lot of money. And he, Francesco, had none and knew that his father would never buy one. It wasn't only the engine which was expensive, it would also cost money to use it. A donkey, on the other hand, was cheap. Even if he only got thorns to eat, he would go on patiently pulling the beam round and round.

There was silence while old Thomas smoked his blackened pipe and watched a pair of seagulls as they circled, screaming. Francesco was thoughtfully drawing the outlines of an engine in the sand.

'I can let you have an engine,' said the fisherman unexpectedly. 'It would have to be completely taken to bits, of course, and thoroughly cleaned. It's old, but it's still usable. I'll help you do the work, I know a bit about it.'

Francesco's eyes sparkled with happiness. He looked gratefully at Thomas but he couldn't say a word.

'Francesco, you should be getting home now. We'll talk about it again tomorrow,' said the old fisherman and he picked up his wooden needle.

'Will the engine be expensive?' asked Francesco anxiously.

'No, my boy. Don't worry about that. We'll do it together. The engine needs new plugs and one or two other things. You can help me to mend my nets in your free time and come out to sea with me sometimes to help me with my fishing. You'll earn what you need that way.'

'That's wonderful, Thomas! Thanks very much! I'll go and tell Sfortunata at once,' cried Francesco eagerly and tore off on his bicycle. He was blissful! All he had to do to earn the engine was mend nets and help with the fishing. There was nothing he would rather do. He stamped down on the pedals, eager to get back and talk to his father as quickly as possible. He wanted to tell him that he was going to earn the engine by his own work, earn it like a grown-up. But suddenly Francesco decided not to tell his father anything about the engine. He might forbid him to do it. The engine would remain his and Thomas's secret and one day it would be a big surprise.

But Francesco did want to ask his father's permission to tie a cloth over Sfortunata's eyes and allow her to trot beside her mother. Then she would not be alone while he, Francesco, was

working on the engine or helping old
Thomas to fish.

6 A Good Plan Goes Wrong

Next morning, almost before the sun had appeared in the sky, the Corsicans began work at the olive press. Trotella was one of the first at work. Secured to the heavy beam, she trotted round and round in circles, her eyes covered, humble and obedient.

Two hours later, Francesco went to see Sfortunata in her stable. He wanted to take her to the press, to follow her mother round with the beam. His father had given him permission. He tied a cloth gently over

Sfortunata's eyes and guided her, full
of hope, to the olive press.

Sfortunata was happy and Francesco hoped she would keep going for a
long time. When they arrived the
hands looked up in surprise and began

to snigger quietly. Only Francesco's father was not laughing. He loved his son more than anything else in the world, but Francesco's soft heart didn't please him. He watched the two in silence and wondered what was going to become of his dreamy son. Francesco had always dreamed of becoming a fisherman or a shepherd. He always wanted to live in the open and have animals about him, and that didn't appeal to his father at all. He wanted to make his son into a sturdy farmer, or an artisan. But Francesco showed neither pleasure nor interest, on the contrary he was always demonstrating his lack of sense and skill.

Meanwhile, little Sfortunata was trotting beside her mother, head held high, touching her from time to time with the busy paintbrush of her tail, just as she had the day before. But Trotella did not return her caress. Francesco noticed at once and wondered anxiously what it meant. Yesterday, when the little donkey had escaped from the stable and trotted beside her mother, Trotella had returned the caress tenderly. But today? Isn't she pleased to have her baby with her? Francesco wondered in bewilderment. He had been quite sure that the mother donkey would be as glad as her little one, but Trotella sensed that this idea would not really help Sfortunata. Francesco had meant well, of course, but the experienced donkey knew that Sfortunata was not strong enough to keep up this monotonous circling for long, even with her eyes bound.

The farmhands, constantly pouring olives into the press and carrying away the resulting oil, grinned at the odd sight. Soon they were making bets.

'Sfortunata won't hold out for more than twenty turns,' said one. Another thought she would manage at least thirty turns and yet another went so far as to bet that she would hold out for fifty turns.

At first Sfortunata accompanied her mother willingly, although the sun was already quite high in the sky. It was autumn, but the sun was hot; Corsica is a warm, southern island. It was hot, even standing still in the sun, and all the more so if you had to go round and round in circles all the time. Sfortunata was too tired. Her tongue seemed to grow longer, hanging from her mouth as a dog's does in high summer, when he is thirsty. It was more and more of an effort for her to put one foot in front of the other. Trotella became restless. She felt that her little one was in trouble. She too began to go slowly and was scolded. Sfortunata seemed to be trying to pull herself together, but her little legs would no longer obey her. As on the day before, she dragged on for another two rounds and fell, first to her knees and then to the ground. At that moment Trotella stopped dead and began to bray heart-breakingly.

Francesco was bitterly disappointed when he saw Sfortunata lying on the ground and heard her mother's plaintive cry. It was only now that he understood Trotella's strange behaviour. She had known from the start that this experiment would end badly. Francesco was unhappy. He hurried over to Sfortunata, knelt on the ground beside her and stroked her head and neck, whispering loving words in her ear. He told her about the engine which he was going to repair with Thomas to set her free. He told her of green meadows in which she would soon be able to play all day long, and of tasty food which she would eat. But she heard none of the comforting words; her tremendous effort had left her unconscious. Francesco looked around helplessly. Then his father came over, picked the unlucky one up in his arms and carried her silently to the stable. Francesco followed him.

There was silence around the olive press. None of the men was laughing now. Francesco made up his mind that he was going to start work on the engine the very next morning. At first he thought he might be able to repair it in the stable so that Sfortunata need not be alone, but he rejected that idea at once. He wanted the engine to be a surprise to his father, the farmhands and the whole village.

Moreover, he knew only too well that he would not get far without Thomas's help, and Thomas would never be able to spend many hours in the stable. He had to go out fishing every night for the sake of his big family and take his catch to market and sell it next day. Thomas also had to mend and wash his nets and drink wine with the other fishermen in the village pub.

Francesco thought. Suddenly he realised that he was lying beside Sfortunata in the straw and that they were alone in the stable. Where had his father gone? Francesco had not even noticed when he had left, he had been so absorbed in his thoughts. He had not even thanked him for carrying Sfortunata to the stable.

Sfortunata seemed to be sleeping. Now and again her long ears or her thin little legs twitched. It was only then that Francesco noticed that the cloth was still tied over her eyes. He undid it carefully, anxious not to wake her. She had valiantly earned her sleep. But what was to be done for the little donkey while he and Thomas were putting the engine to rights?

Francesco had been sitting beside Sfortunata in the hay for a long time before the solution came to him. Suddenly he had it: he would fence in an area of green pasture with wire netting and make a playground for Sfortunata. She would be able to sun herself in there and enjoy the good autumn air, instead of being frightened in the gloomy stable. Francesco planned to build the enclosure close to the olive press so that Sfortunata could watch her mother working. This wonderful plan filled his heart with warmth and hope. He lay down contentedly in the hay, picturing to himself how Sfortunata would dance in her enclosure and watch other animals at play: the eagles circling high in the sky, the peevish gulls, the red-brown squirrels and the cheerful birds. Above all, she would be able to watch her mother. That was how Francesco pictured his four-legged friend's future, in beautiful colours. It was not long before his pleasure and the scent of the hay had lulled him to sleep.

7 Francesco and his Father

In the morning, when the first rays of sunshine turned the crown of the old nut tree to gold, Francesco awakened. He was surprised to find himself in his own bed, not in the stable. When and how had he come into the house? He remembered nothing. His father came into the room and Francesco gave him a beaming 'Good morning!' Then his father told him that he had been found with the little donkey in the stable after the whole house had been searched without success. He had been

44

lying beside Sfortunata in the hay,
sleeping peacefully. There was no hint
of reproach in his father's voice and
Francesco was encouraged to talk
enthusiastically about his plan to

45

build Sfortunata an enclosure where she could sun herself, graze and play under the blue sky.

At first Francesco's father would not even consider this new fancy of his son's, but then it occurred to him that Francesco might learn something through it. So when he approved the plan, it was just because he doubted his son's ability to work with his hands. But there was one condition: the boy had to do the work entirely on his own, measure the area, select and cut the posts and drive them into the ground. After that he would have to pick out the right wire, cut it, nail it and do everything else that was needed. However, Sfortunata's pasture was on no account to be anywhere near the olive press. 'It will soon be the rainy season and all the olives have to be pressed by then. No one must disturb Trotella's work,' said his father firmly. 'There's no good pasture there, either,' he added and left the room.

Francesco was satisfied. He thought his father's conditions were quite fair;

after all, he wanted his Sfortunata to
have rich pasture on which she could
graze to her heart's content.

Francesco got up, filled with hope,
and went to the kitchen. The maid,
Rosalia, gave him his breakfast. His
mother had died before he had learned

47

to walk and he no longer remembered her. He was attached to the kindly maid, who had looked after the house for his grandmother and was one of the family. He told her excitedly about his plan. Rosalia understood him very well and was glad that Francesco loved animals. She was particularly glad that he loved the shaggy little Long Ears. She kissed his sunburnt forehead and sent him off to the stable.

Sfortunata was still asleep. Softly, softly, in order not to waken her, Francesco got out the tools he needed: a pick and shovel, an axe, a roll of wire, a hammer, pincers and nails of various sizes. Then he quickly selected the spot. Every hour was important for little Sfortunata.

8 Francesco Sets to Work

Francesco had chosen a beautiful pasture for his shaggy little friend's enclosure, a patch of juicy grass at the edge of the wood.

The work went well. Digging the holes in the ground was easier than Francesco had imagined and soon the posts were in position. Bang-bang went the hammer, as Francesco fixed the wire netting. He had not even forgotten to make a door, although that had been quite hard work, but Francesco did it willingly because it was for his beloved Sfortunata.

Soon curious inhabitants of the woodland gathered to watch. The sparrows were the first, eager to see if they could slip through the holes in the netting. And after the sparrows had hopped in and out of the enclosure, the tits and finches came to join in. They cocked their heads on one side and peered with curious, beady eyes at what Francesco was doing. Sometimes they would whistle a little tune or fly up sharply when Francesco banged too loudly with the hammer.

Francesco was so absorbed in his work that he did not even notice his inquisitive visitors. Soon Sfortunata would be able to exchange her gloomy stable for the sunny pasture, he thought happily, and worked on with a will.

When the sun was three quarters of the way across the sky, Francesco had finished his work. All that was missing from the enclosed pasture was its guest. Francesco gathered up his tools, spared a last look for the enclosure and prepared to leave. At that moment his father appeared and Francesco realised that he had missed his lunch. He expected his father to scold him and apologised at once, but his father had no such thought. He tested all the posts carefully to make sure that they would stand up to any gales. He inspected the door of the enclosure thoroughly and assured himself that the wire was firmly secured and the fence high enough. Silently he was admiring Francesco's work and feeling proud of his son. It was a well-planned and well executed piece of work, which would stand up to all weathers. Francesco's father congratulated him and they returned to the house together. When they reached the stable Francesco went off to see Sfortunata. His father had no more objections; he was only amazed that a donkey should have aroused his dreamy son.

Francesco fetched Sfortunata and led her to her new pasture.

9 Sfortunata Has Some Cheerful Visitors

Francesco was very pleased with his enclosure, but Sfortunata was not. Francesco had strewn golden-yellow oats inside it for her, and they are party food for any donkey in the world,

but Sfortunata would not touch them.

Sfortunata was obviously disappointed. She must have been expecting Francesco to take her to her mother. 'What am I supposed to do in this lonely spot?' she thought and walked restlessly up and down her enclosure, like a captive tiger. She was constantly trying to find a hole through which to escape. She did not spare a glance for the golden-yellow oats. If only she had stopped trying to plan hopeless flight and looked to the north, where a long olive grove made a silver streak of colour! It was a beautiful silver grey, such as you see only in Corsica.

Sfortunata could have seen a wonderful sight in the east as well. That was where the magnificent forest of macchia flourished, a wealth of indescribable colour. But the little donkey would only trot round and round, snuffling at the wire and trying to jump the fence, which was so high that even a wild pony would not have been able to jump it. Francesco had made it high

on purpose. He knew his stubborn little donkey!

It was a long time before Sfortunata seemed to be calming down. She looked about her, stared at the yellow oats and suddenly began to gobble them. Francesco took advantage of this to leave, because he knew now that Sfortunata would soon feel at home in her pasture. It was so beautiful by the edge of the wood, under the high arch of the sky.

'She should be happy,' said Francesco, and hurried off to see Thomas. He wanted to tell him about his success with the enclosure and begin on his next job at once.

When Sfortunata had had enough of her golden oats, she licked her lips contentedly, a sure sign that they had tasted good. A moment later she had a visitor. The birds were the first guests, twittering cheerfully in the trees as if they were putting on a concert for the little donkey. The sparrows had been hopping to and fro through the netting for some time and Sfortunata liked their company. Then the pig family from the farmyard came along: mother sow with her five comical piglets, grunting all the time and looking up at Sfortunata now and then with their slitty eyes. And who was this flying past? A huge eagle circled soundlessly above the meadow. Soon afterwards there was a crackling in the twigs at the edge of the wood. A bright red squirrel leaped down into the grass, hopped over to the playground, and suddenly a nut was roll-

ing into the enclosure. Sfortunata sniffed at it, but she would not eat it. She knew about thistles and thorns, but she would have to ask her mother before she was sure that donkeys could eat hard things like this. On the other hand, the round object was fun to play with. She could roll it around with her feet—that was a good game—but soon she stopped playing with the nut and looked up at the sky again to admire the giant eagle. It filled her with amazement; she had never seen such an enormous bird before.

All the other little birds were twittering in the stillness of the late afternoon, as if to pass on the news of young Long Ears to all the inhabitants of the wood. A deer peeped shyly from the bushes and hesitantly approached the enclosure. Soon afterwards the brown mare trotted over from the meadow with her inquisitive foal. A lot of curious creatures were gathered around Sfortunata's playground by the edge of the wood!

Meanwhile Francesco and Thomas

were working on the engine and getting on quickly. They were happy, and Sfortunata was happy to be in this delightful place after her gloomy stable.

10 Fear at the Edge of the Wood

Sfortunata the baby donkey was having more and more fun in her little pasture with all her visitors, and the visitors were having more and more fun with the little donkey and beginning to make friends with each other. But in the midst of this happy time all the animals suddenly started up. The sparrow shot into the enclosure like an arrow, landed between Sfortunata's big ears and was immediately hidden. The other birds flew like lightning into the thickness of the wood. The foal landed with one leap between her mother's strong legs. The pink piglets waddled to their mother and hid under her round belly. Even the big animals ducked and looked anxiously towards the sky, but the eagle continued to circle with majestic calm.

At first Sfortunata had no idea what had happened. What was all this panic about? But then she noticed something black streaking down from the sky and she too felt frightened and

would have liked to run to her mother for shelter. What was it streaking across the sky, a stone or some terrible enemy?

No, it was neither a stone nor an enemy; it was only a jackdaw, nothing but a jet-black jackdaw with a yellow beak. Now it was spreading its wings to circle twice over Sfortunata's playground before landing calmly on one of the posts. When the startled animals saw the jackdaw they sighed with relief and stopped being afraid. The little birds came back and chattered crossly, as if they were scolding the jackdaw. But really they were glad that it was not a predatory hawk, as they had feared at first. The foal watched the jackdaw for a while and then began to play again; the pink piglets ventured out and stood in a row like soldiers, eyeing the black bird. 'How can anything be so black!' grunted the piglets. And what did the sparrow do? He behaved as importantly as if he had never known the meaning of fear and had only wanted

64

to play with Sfortunata.

Sfortunata was pleased that everything was peaceful again. She loved her playground, but if there were danger she would rather have been with her mother. Now everything was all right again. She looked curiously at the jackdaw. What was it doing on her post? Nothing in particular. The jackdaw looked at Sfortunata, measuring her from her long ears to her hooves, and then it had gone, flown away.

Why was it in such a hurry? Was it a messenger from the valleys to the mountains? Was it flying off to spread the news of the little Long Ears in the meadow?

Finches and tits began to twitter their cheerful songs again and the sparrow chirped out long, long stories to entertain Sfortunata.

Towards evening, when Sfortunata was grazing peacefully and her other visitors were romping round the enclosure, they suddenly all stared towards a certain rock as if a spell had been cast over them. 'Now what's the mat-

ter?' wondered the little donkey. High up on the rock stood a red-gold fox! He was taking a critical look at Long Ears in her pasture. He did not trust it, the whole thing was obviously a trap. He was very mistrustful by nature and lived at enmity with human beings. The little donkey did not know who this late visitor was, but she was glad when he did not come any closer. His face frightened her and she longed for the comforting presence of her mother. But luckily the wild creature did not stay long; after a few moments he vanished back into the thicket as soundlessly as he had come.

After this mysterious visit it soon grew dark. Francesco took his shaggy friend back to her stable, where her mother was already waiting impatiently for her.

That night, when Sfortunata had drunk her fill of her mother's milk and felt warm and safe, she told her mother all about her experiences at the edge of the wood.

11 Sfortunata Takes Fish to Market

So the days and weeks passed. Sfortunata was no longer a baby donkey, but she continued to graze in her enclosure. She played with the sparrows, listened to the twittering of the birds or slept in the soft grass, all four legs comfortably outstretched. Now and again she played with the foal as it performed its tricks beyond the fence, which Sfortunata tried to imitate.

Meanwhile Francesco was hard at work on his engine, and helping old Thomas to mend nets and above all to

fish. They often brought home a fine
catch and when that happened Francesco would fetch his Sfortunata and
take her down to see Thomas. Then the

two of them, the bearded fisherman and Francesco his assistant, loaded the full baskets on Sfortunata's back and the three of them would walk to the little town of St. Florent to sell the fish in the market.

Sfortunata loved those days. They were quite different from the days in the dark stable or in her playground by the wood. She was glad to be able to help. Also she made friends with other donkeys in the market and enjoyed a chat with them.

Francesco always put part of his share from the sales of fish into a wooden money box which he had made himself and kept hidden in the stable, just where Sfortunata slept. This was the money for the engine parts which had to be replaced.

'Sfortunata is growing faster than my work on the engine,' thought Francesco, but he was soothed by the thought that the olive press would have an engine one day and Sfortunata would be released for ever from the dull, hard work at the press. His donkey would never have to pull the heavy beam from early morning till late at night, as her mother had done year after year. And if Sfortunata had a foal it would not have to be left alone in the gloomy stable; no, Sfortunata would be able to look after it, feed it and play with it, as the brown mare did with her foal. Trotella would not have to go on with her hard labour in her old age, either.

But Francesco's father was not at all pleased with his son. He knew nothing of Francesco's work or his money box, and he did not like his son to spend so much time with Thomas and out at sea. Still, he let him go, because he hoped that one day Francesco would see how hard a fisherman's work is and how little money it brings in. He hoped that this would make his son stop wanting to be a fisherman himself. But Francesco knew nothing of his father's worries. He was happy and he worked on his engine like a madman.

12 Freedom

The months were passing and once again the trees were laden with fruit. The woods began to turn gold, the grapes were ripe, a soft wind blew over the meadows and the water. It was autumn again on the island of Corsica.

Francesco worked on the old engine as if he were unable to stop. He must work with all his might now, because Sfortunata had grown into a strong donkey and she was to be put to the heavy beam. There were lots of olives

to be pressed and Trotella had been hired out to another farmer. All the work was just waiting for Sfortunata.

Francesco was to be sent to the town, too, to learn a trade. He had been apprenticed to a carpenter in St. Florent. Francesco did all he could to put off his departure by a few days, but his father was getting very angry because he was convinced that Francesco still wanted to be a fisherman and was resisting the idea of learning a craft. So he fixed the day and hour of Francesco's departure. He was to leave his village next Sunday, in a week's time. Francesco agreed. He was sure that his engine would be ready in three days. There was not much left to do.

The following Thursday, Sfortunata would be pulling the heavy beam of the olive press for the first time, just as her mother had done, year in, year out, from early morning till late at night.

Francesco and Thomas worked on the engine from morning till night and on Wednesday night they set it up in secret near the press. They connected

74

the beam to the engine with a leather strap and waited for the great moment.

In the grey dawn, when thick mist still hung over the countryside and the olive press, the hired helpers and Francesco's father arrived. The last to come was old Dominic, pulling the unhappy Sfortunata on a rope behind him. The men brought basket after basket of ripe olives and set them

down close to the press. When they went off to fetch new basketfuls, Francesco and Thomas stole up, under cover of the mist, and started the engine. Then the heavy beam began to turn, as if it were as light as a feather.

The farmhands' eyes opened wide in astonishment. Even Francesco's father could scarcely believe what he was seeing. It seemed to all of them as if they were witnessing a miracle!

Hidden behind a bush, Thomas and Francesco watched the astonished faces with delight before showing themselves. They told the helpers to pour olives into the press, because they wanted to prove what good work their engine could do. Of course it was ten times stronger than a donkey and worked ten times as fast.

When Francesco's father learnt from Thomas what had been going on, he was almost wild with joy. His son, that dreamy lad, had put an engine in working order! 'My Francesco, my Francesco!' he cried again and again, not sure if he were dreaming or if it were all really true. He was immeasurably proud of his son and kept on asking old Thomas: 'Was it really my Francesco, my dreamy lad, who got the idea of repairing an engine?'

And Thomas smiled and nodded and had to tell the farmer and the assembled hands the whole story all over again, from the beginning until this most happy day.

There were high spirits around the olive press as well, beaming faces, joy and laughter. Butterflies tumbled drunkenly about, birds fluttered round the turning press and sang their loveliest songs.

Francesco sat blissfully at the edge of the wood, so happy that all he wanted to do was sit on the grass and watch the festivities, and Sfortunata. Francesco's father was overjoyed. 'What did I tell you?' said old Rosalia. 'A tender heart has its uses. . . .'

Francesco wanted to be a mechanic now, to make so many engines that all the donkeys in the islands of Corsica, Sardinia and Sicily could be released from the heavy beams of the olive presses. His proud father was in complete agreement and ordered old Dominic to bring out the wine.

Soon a village feast was in full swing by the olive press, instead of the usual strenuous work. Farmers and farmhands came pouring in from the countryside to see the 'magic engine' and taste the good wine. And while everyone was drinking and singing, the olive press went steadily on working. The engine turned the heavy beam as though it were a pleasure to press the precious oil out of the ripe olives all day long. The farmers decorated engine and press with autumn flowers and the farmers' wives made a garland for Sfortunata.

The party went on for many hours. Francesco and Thomas were happy. Francesco's father was happy. And Sfortunata was not the unlucky one now; she had become Fortunata, the lucky one, the happiest of them all.